Education

"Education is a necessary tool in life, it is needed to help shape ones attitude and latitude. Education is a tool that carves out ignorance in the building blocks of society and can be used to market ones capabilities."

Dr. Ronald E. White, Sr.

Critical Thinking for Critical Times in a Non-Profit World takes a look at a very complex concept and simplifies it, so that the least informed on the subject comes away with a good understanding. I recommend it for anyone interested in learning how critical thinking can impact their personal and professional lives.

Former Ambassador Kolby Koomson, Ghana; President, The Koomson Group, Inc.

"A stimulating, provocative and thoughtful book.... *Critical Thinking For Critical Times In a Non-Profit World* is a book you will want to read."

-*Ronnie Williams, VP for Student Services, University of Central Arkansas*

CRITICAL THINKING
FOR CRITICAL TIMES
In a Non-Profit World

Decisions, decisions, decisions Non-profit organizations face all kinds of situations that require a decision, but do they know what to do to make the best possible decision?

Ronald E White

Divine Publishing

Published by
Divine Publishing
Conway, Arkansas

Copyright © 2006 Ronald E. White

All rights reserved. No part of this book may be reproduced in any form, except for the inclusion of brief quotations in review, without permission in writing from the author or publisher.

Library Congress card number 2006923308

ISBN 0-9779170-0-2

First Edition Spring 2006

Text editing by: Rebecca Hayes

Printed in the United States by
Instant Publisher
410 West Highway 72
Collierville, Tennessee 38017

Acknowledgements

Special Thanks
To
Dr. Michael Rubach,
Mr. Max Dyer, and
God Almighty

Dedication

To my beautiful wife, Sheila, and our 5 beautiful children,
Lorenzo, Shaquinetta, Ronald Jr., Elijah, and Abigail

To the students I have had the
privilege of instructing.

To my sister and her husband
(Raymond and Yvonne Farmer),
Jim and Deanna Downey
(Thanks for the encouragement)

Last, but certainly not least, all of the Men and Woman who
dedicate their lives in helping others.

Coming Soon!

Contact the author about workshops and seminars developed from this book .

rw318@juno.com

Table of Contents

Introduction 1

Chapter 1 What Is A Non-profit Organization? 3

Chapter 2 Non-profit vs. For-Profit 5

Other Differences 6

Chapter3 Financial Management Of Non-Profits 9

Financial Managers Guidelines 9

The Board of Directors 10

Chapter 4 Non-profit Leadership 17

Leadership: 17

Effective Leaders 18

Chapter 5 What Is Critical Thinking? 19

Chapter 6 What's Critical About Critical Thinking? 24

Decision-Making 24

Importance Of Critical Thinking 25

Chapter 7 Elements Of Critical Thinking 28

Mental Modals for Guiding the Thinking process 29

Conclusion: 29

Chapter 8 Critical Thinking Skills 32

Systematic Decision making 32

Eight Steps in Systematic Decision-Making 32

Intuition 33

Creativity 33

Chapter 9 Influences On Critical Thinking 36

Ethics 36

Gender 37

Economical Status 37

Conclusion: 37

Chapter 10 Challenges Faced By Non-Profit Organizations
.... 40

Fundraising and Fees 41

Recruiting & orienting quality of service: 45

Conclusion 46

Chapter 11 Strategic Planning In The Non-profit Sector. 48

Resource misallocation *50*

Conclusion *52*

References 54

Glossary 58

Critical Thinking for Critical Times

Introduction

Decisions, decisions, decisions. Non-profit organizations face all kinds of situations that require a decision, but do they know what to do to make the best possible decision? Do they know the forces that influence their decisions? Decision-making is more than a choice between A and B. It requires learned critical thinking skills and an awareness of how decisions can be influenced.

After years of working in the Non-Profit and For- Profit world, I have found that decision-making skills are sometimes lacking. Critical thinking is therefore not an easy process to define. However, it is important to focus on each individual component of the concept and grasp it properly in order to understand the critical thinking process on the whole. While there is no unanimously accepted definition of critical thinking, educators and researchers have agreed on some of the important components of the concept, which can help us develop the habit and ability of thinking critically.

Critical thinking involves careful evaluation of information, serious and complete unbiased reflection, and it must be accompanied with a sincere desire to reach objective results. Objectivity is the most important mental attribute that one needs to develop or possess in order to become a critical thinker. Biased opinion and clouded thinking interfere with the process of critical thinking and for this reason emotions must not be allowed to affect one's ability to think critically.

This is my attempt to cause the reader to challenge him or herself to take a look at the skills that are being applied at their organization and the consequent process of change.

Ronald E. White, Sr.

Chapter 1

What Is A Non-profit Organization?

The primary objective of forming a non-profit organization is to provide services to the community. The term "non-profit" is used for those types of business that are formed on the principle that profits will not be distributed to the owners. The majority of the non-profit organizations are organized under the legal cover of corporations; which are formed under the corporation law of the state in which they are operating. States have their own statutes regulating the formation of non-profit corporations; some allow for formation of other forms of organizations such as trusts or unincorporated associations. The Internal Revenue Service (IRS) has exempted those organizations from taxes under section 501. If the organizations serve any kind of charitable, religious, scientific, or educational purposes they are generally exempt from federal income taxes. The typical structure of a non-profit organization includes three major characteristics, these are:

(1) Control,

(2) Programs and
(3) Central Administration

The *control* or governance function of a non-profit organization is responsible for overall strategic planning, decision-making, guidance and control of the organization. Effective governance is necessary to keep the activities of the organization in line with its objectives. Moreover, the goals and objectives defined by the top management of the non-profit organizations are to be materialized. This can be done through effective utilization of resources, owned by the organization, to organize different *programs* for the benefit of the society. The success of these programs is then measured in terms of their outcomes. Outcomes are usually measured by analyzing the impact of organization's services on the society. Finally, to keep the functions of the organization running, it employs some expert staff in its *central administration*. As non-profit organizations are limited in terms of resources, they should try to keep the cost of hiring administrative personnel as low as possible. This issue is itself a challenge for many non-profit organizations.

Footnotes
References

Kent E. Dove: Conducting a Successful Capital Campaign: The New, Revised and
Expanded Edition of the Leading Guide to Planning and Implementing a Capital
Campaign: Jossey-Bass: 2nd edition: October 1999
Stanley Weinstein & Robert F. Hartsook: The Complete Guide to Fund-Raising
Management: John Wiley & Sons: 2nd edition: February 2002
Michael Allison & Jude Kaye: Strategic Planning for Non-profit Organizations:
A Practical Guide and Workbook: John Wiley & Sons: July 1997

Chapter 2

Non-profit vs. For-Profit

Non-profit organizations do things somewhat differently than *for-profit* organizations; this is especially true when it comes to how they manage their finances and how they provide their financial information to others. Naturally, these non-profit organizations have to make money, or they would not be able to remain in business and help others. However they do not make their money for a profit. There are no investors on quarterly bases to whom to report, no dividends to distribute. Instead, non-profits take their money and turn it back into goods and services that benefit their target populations, pay their employees, and pay their bills. As to be expected, they must show their cash flow and they must also show what kind of financial statements they have. However they do not provide the same type of financial documentation that for-profit organizations do. They are also treated differently where taxes are concerned, and are under different accounting rules.

Looking at these issues in-depth is not necessary. Instead, a basic overview will be provided that will give insight into the non-profit vs..for-profit organizations, their similarities and differences. This will help in drawing of conclusions about non-profit organizations and where they are headed. This is important, because many non-profit organizations have been accused of making too much money, while others seem to struggle with what they are able to do for themselves and for others. Non-profit organizations are facing some critical times, with natural disasters, the current war situation, the cost of gas, and the simple fact that people in general are very cautious about giving.

This environment is a concern for not only those struggling organizations, but also for the individuals and groups that those organizations help.

Without non-profit organizations, there would be less help for those that need it most, and there would not be enough to go around for those individuals that are struggling for assistance. This is especially true when natural disasters (such as hurricane Katrina) and other problems strike. The main concern that some have over non-profit organizations making too much money hinges on the fact that the directors of some of the largest non-profit organizations make six-figure salaries. This seems to be a bit much for the director of a company that is not supposed to be making a profit, but instead supposed to be helping others with their problems in times of need.

Other Differences

For the next chapter, it is important to look at and review Financial Management, the importance of having a proactive Board of Directors. It is important to see the similarities and differences when it comes to a comparison between non-profit organizations and for-profit organizations. This comparison will help to give more insight into non-profit organizations and allow the reader to proceed into an analysis of what has been learned. By analyzing and evaluating non-profit organizations using critical thinking, conclusions can be drawn and recommendations can be made about what has been learned.

Critical Thinking for Critical Times 9

Chapter3

Financial Management Of Non-Profits

Reviewing past documentation is always very important, and in this chapter it will be brief. There is much that should be and has been said about non-profit organizations and their financial management, but limited space allows only the basic information to be imparted here. Non-profit organizations are very interested in achieving their missions and goals, and in order to do this they often work toward them very strongly, paying little to no regard to their financial management, which presents many challenges for their managers.

There are certain things that financial managers must be concerned with and pay close attention to. When dealing with non-profit organizations, many of these things differ from for-profit organizations. These include:

Financial Managers Guidelines

1) **Understanding the mission statement.**
2) **Executing the mission with compassion and full commitment**

3) **Researching, Researching, Researching, your field of operation. (Who are your clientele, what are their demographics, the average income in your area etc...)**
4) **Defining and understanding success.**
5) **Making sure that the financial managers understands that the non-profit organization wants to experience long-term success.**
6) **Recognizing how important and vital a board of directors can be to a non-profit organization.**
7) **Learning to accept a certain amount of risk.**

All of these issues have a great deal of significance for the financial management of a non-profit organization. There are many strong differences between non-profits and for-profit organizations that they resemble each other on the surface. Tax-exempt status is one of the major differences. As charitable organizations many non-profit organizations are exempt from paying taxes. However, this is a privilege, not a right. It can be easily revoked if the non-profit organization is not meeting all of the guidelines for charitable purposes that are set out by the IRS.

The Board of Directors

Having an active board of directors is very important for a non-profit organization. The issues faced by the different management and financial management are very different than a for-profit company. There are five specific financial risks that must be managed in a proactive manner by the board of directors. These are:

1) The cost of lost opportunities,
2) Financial crunches,
3) Uncontrollable costs,

Critical Thinking for Critical Times 11

4) Increased difficulty with recognizing revenues that meet forecasts, and
5) The lack of a successful model for management.

Not all non-profit organizations realize just how important their boards of directors are. If the board is able to manage the above five risks in a proactive way, the board will insure the future stability of the organization. In order to be strategically instrumental in their organizational missions, boards must realize that they cannot simply sit back and wait until some kind of crisis arises. Instead, they must anticipate problems before they get started, and therefore keep the organization running along smoothly.

Protecting the organization against being financially misused is very significant. Since there are some non-profit workers who will try to use and abuse the organization, the board must work diligently to prevent employees profiting own personal gain. There are individuals like this all over the world, and non-profit organizations must continuously safeguard themselves against it as much as possible. Many organizations think that it cannot happen to them, but it can, and does. There are several steps that can be taken, however, to protect a non-profit organization. These include:

1. Admitting that there could be misuse in one's own organization,
2. Letting all employees know that this is something that is taken very seriously,
3. Making sure that one is willing to ask hard questions,
4. Let several individuals share the financial balance-checking load , and
5 . Get help from professionals to safeguard the organization as much as possible.

Non-profit organizations must watch their finances carefully. They are required to offer a statement of activities, and a statement of financial position. There are also other financial statements that the non-profit organization must provide, such as the statement of functional expenses and the statement of cash flows, as well as the financial statement disclosures.

Non-profit organizations often do not spend enough time dealing with financial issues because they are so focused on their missions that they are sworn to uphold. However, without paying attention to the financial issues, these organizations can run into real trouble. They need to orient themselves to the financial workings of their organization, and they need to develop a realistic budget that works well for all people involved. Without a realistic budget, the organization will likely not succeed, because there will be constant struggle and upset regarding whether issues such as bills are dealt with efficiently and properly to ensure that the organization keeps running.

Non-profit vs. for-profit organizations, while different are becoming somewhat blurred. There have been more complaints in the last 20 years or so because the non-profit sector has begun to insert itself more and more into the market economy. Distinguishing the differences based on intent is sometimes difficult. Taking advantage of this ambiguous system is not uncommon practice for many organizations.

Pricing has become a concern in recent years because of the fact that non-profit organizations often charge different prices to different individuals, based on need. There are generally strict rules in the for-profit sector about charging everyone the same price (Robinson-Patman Act), but the non-profit sector looks at things somewhat differently. Accounting is another area where there are important differences when looking at for-profit and non-profit corporations. Generally, it is believed that there are four specific differences:

1. Accounting for contributions,
2. Capitalizing and depreciating assets,
3. Functional expense classification, and
4. Use of both cash- and modified-cash basis accounting methods.

These accounting differences and methods are not important, however, if the non-profit organization cannot analyze and maintain its finances, serious problems can arise. Missions are very important for non-profit organizations, as well they should be, but without successful financial management, the mission will usually fail. Proper financial management requires the utilization of trend analysis to see where a non-profit organization has been, without knowing where you have been, it's difficult for the organization to take a good look at where it is going. These two things together can often show a non-profit organization whether it is on track in accomplishing its mission.

Another thing that must be examined when looking at the similarities and differences between for-profit and non-profit organizations is the intent. In other words, the idea of operating as a non-profit organization must be intentional. A company that makes no profit for a period of one year cannot claim non-profit status. Even some hospitals that pay all of their bills out of what their patients pay them may not be considered non-profit, depending upon how they were created and how they have been run in the past. Those that receive goods or services from a non-profit organization are similar to the customers that a for-profit organization would have.

Key financial roles in non-profit organizations fall into three distinct categories. Knowing what these are and where everyone fits is one of the crucial elements of understanding non-profit financial management. There are three key financial roles:

Key Roles

1. The auditor's role.
2. The management role.
3. The board's role.

The role of the *Auditors* is a crucial role, in light of the Sarbanes-Oxley act of 2002, an act that came about because of the lack of self-governance by For-Profit organizations. Auditors should have total independence; managerial functions must not be performed by auditors, nor any activity that may later require auditing. Here are a few things that a Non-Profit Organization should consider:

- The audit committee should have a charter that includes appropriate role and authority language.
- Avoid compensation of audit committee members and make sure they have no financial interest in, or conflict of interest with, companies the organization does business with.
- Members of the audit committee must be independent, and management should not be voting members of the audit committee.

The role of *Management* is to oversee daily operations of the organization. It is the responsibility of management to provide ethical and effective leadership, along with budget planning, financial reporting and risk management.

The role of the *Board* members is not to become involved in the daily operations of a nonprofit, but rather should develop the standards of organizational behavior by which operations will be conducted by senior management and others.

Not only do these respective roles have significance, but possibly the most significant issue comes from looking at matching personnel and determining which individual fits into what role and what must be done in each one of these roles. Some of the duties of these various roles overlap to a certain extent. However, for the most part, they are separate and the individuals that work in each specific role must be aware not only of what they need to be doing but what others are supposed to be doing as well. If someone makes a mistake or is not doing his or her job, this can be noticed and corrected before it affects the entire organization. It is also important that individuals are placed into these types of roles very carefully because the possibility for stealing money and causing other problems for the company is very great. Individuals that are in positions of superiority or that are working with the financial future of the company, may be prone to this does not mean to imply that all of these individuals are thieves or that all of them will attempt to cause difficulties. However, the non-profit organizations that are not aware of the idea that it can happen to them often find that it has and they are not aware of how to deal with it or how it occurred in the first place.

Foot-notes:

Alliance (2004). FAQ. Alliance for Risk Management. http://www.allianceon line.org/FAQ/risk_management/what_are_most_common_1.faq

Analysis of FASB 117. (2003). The Non Profit Resource Center. http://www.1800net.com/nprc/fasb117.html

Dennis, A. (1997). Managing with a mission. Journal of Accountancy, 184(4): 71-75.

Fee, D. (2000). Understanding financial operations. Association Management, 52(1): 112-114
Goehner, D. (1999). Protecting your organization against financial misuse. Non-profit World, 17(4): 38-39.
Langan, J.P. (1998). Understanding non-profit financial management. Association Management, 50(1): 75.

Little, H.B. (2001). Analyze your finances to ensure your mission. Non-profit World, 19(5): 31-33.

Ruiz, R. (1999). Are you fulfilling your financial trust? Non-profit World, 17(1): 22-

Stout, W. (2001). Measure your use of time. Non-profit World, 19(4): 28-33.

Umapathy, S. (1993). Financial risk management: the board's responsibility. Non-profit World, 11(5): 10-14.

Young, D. R. (1999). Economic decisionmaking by non-profit organizations in a market economy: tensions between mission and market. Case Western Reserve University. Paper presented to the independent sector spring research forum. The National Center on Non-profit Enterprise.
http://www.nationalcne.org/papers/tension.htm

Chapter 4

Non-profit Leadership

Non-profit organizations often have frequent turnover in their leadership. This is due only to the fact of the voluntary nature of much their activities, but also because of the fact that new ideas and fresh outlooks on issues are always welcome. They also are set up legally differently from for-profit organizations, as these non-profits are often created as non-stock entities, where the managers and supporters of the organization actually own it. These managers and supporters are also important in another way, in that how they manage the time that they spend working on and with the organization can directly tie into that organization's success or failure.

Leadership:

Leadership has meaning only in an organizational context, and only in the sense of on managing within a system of inequalities. Superior-subordinate relationships help to define leadership behavior, and the culture in any particular society influences the nature of these relationships. Two leadership roles are common to all societies; the first is the

Charismatic role, or the capability to provide vision and inspiration. This is emphasized by transformational leadership concepts. The ability to influence, and communicate the vision, or mission without hard core tactics. The second is the ***instrumental role***, or the capability to design effective organizational processes, control activities, and meet organizational objectives and deadlines. This describes the functional expectations of a leader as a facilitator some. However, each society determines the relative importance of each role and therefore what makes a good leader.

Cross-cultural research has identified a pattern of characteristics common to effective leaders in these two roles, but these commonalities do not constitute shared traits. They include:

Effective Leaders

Conscientiousness Dependability, achievement orientation, and perseverance within the scope of one's responsibilities

Extroversion Open, accessible attitude, as opposed to remaining insulated from group activities

Dominance Appropriate use of authority in a system of inequalities

Self-confidence Comfort in one's own skills and abilities for managing

Recent research has also suggested that regardless of cultural contingencies, **effective leaders** tend to display **intelligence, energy, emotional stability**, and **openness to experience**. In the international context, this last characteristic encourages cultural sensitivity without ethnocentric imposition.

Chapter 5

What Is Critical Thinking?

The ability to think critically has long been considered the most important trait any student or individual can possess to analyze information and reach unbiased conclusions. Critical thinking is therefore an important subject with educators of all disciplines trying to incorporate this skill in learning methodologies. But in order for someone who understands the concept and to incorporate it effectively, it is important to know what exactly is critical thinking. However, this is not an easy task.

It has been noticed that despite the best efforts of thinkers, educators, and researchers, critical thinking has more or less remained an elusive asset and for this reason, there is no widely accepted definition of the concept. However since the beginning of 20th century, tremendous work has been done in this field and thinkers have developed some important definitions of the concepts. These definitions may not explain what precisely is critical thinking but they offer an insight into the various components of critical thinking.

The first person to offer a sound definition of critical thinking was John Dewey who in 1909 presented a good if not complete definition of critical thinking. This definition has been repeatedly published and republished over the decades. According to Dewey, **critical thinking** is an:

Active, persistent, and careful consideration of any belief or supposed form of knowledge in the light of the grounds that support it and the further conclusion to which it tends".

This definition has served as the foundation for other definitions of critical thinking that were developed later. Dewey's definition is considered valuable since it was the first time someone has used the word active for critical thinking process to distinguish it from traditional ways of thinking.

Critical thinking is an active process, which allows individuals to actively participate in the analysis of information and evaluation of data. Instead of passive process where one reaches conclusions naturally without the aid or involvement of his or her own intellectual faculties, an active process is one where a person participates completely in the evaluation of information in order to reach impartial objective results.

Dewey's definition inspired many similar definitions, however each time thinkers tried to make some additions to the original definition. Chance (1996) simplified the earlier definitions of critical thinking and narrowed the process down to some important steps. According to him, critical thinking was:

"...the ability to analyze facts, generate and organize ideas, defend opinions, make comparisons, draw inferences, evaluate arguments and solve problems".

While this definition is good in its own way, it excludes personal attributes of the thinker, which play an important role in performing all the above steps to conduct critical evaluation. In other words, even if we agree with Chance that critical thinking is simply a combination of the steps mentioned in his definition, we still cannot ignore the role played by the thinker in the process. Not all individuals are

Critical Thinking for Critical Times 21

capable of critical evaluation, which reminds us of the significance of personality or character traits required by a thinker.

Delphi Report (1990) solves this problem for us when it includes the characters traits required for critical thinking in its definition of the concept. The report sheds light on the character traits of a critical thinker when it says: "The ideal critical thinker is habitually **inquisitive, well-informed, trustful of reason, open-minded, flexible, fair-minded in evaluation, honest in facing personal biases, prudent** in making judgments, **willing to reconsider, clear about issues, orderly** in complex matters, **diligent** in seeking relevant information, **reasonable** in selection of criteria, **focused** inquiry, and **persistent** in seeking results which are as precise as the subject and the circumstances of inquiry permit."

Studying the above definition of the concept, we realize that personality or character attributes play an important role in the process of critical thinking. Many subsequent definitions of the concept have focused on the thinker as much as the process when explaining the concept. In most definitions, we notice that the word active is either clearly used or implied for which we are heavily indebted to John Dewey who introduced us to the term. Mayer and Goodchild (1990) define critical thinking as an "...active, systematic process of understanding and evaluating arguments. An argument provides an assertion about the properties of some object or the relationship between two or more objects and evidence to support or refute the assertion. Critical thinkers acknowledge that there is no single correct way to understand and evaluate arguments and that all attempts are not necessarily successful."

Similarly Richard Paul and Michael Scriven also define critical thinking as an active process saying that, "Critical thinking is the intellectually disciplined process of actively and skillfully conceptualizing, applying, analyzing, synthesizing, and/or evaluating information gathered from, or generated by, observation, experience, reflection, reasoning, or communication, as a guide to belief and action." Richard Paul and Michael Scriven. While there definition is comprehensive in nature, it borrows from Robert Ennis definition of critical thinking, which has not been widely accepted and has often been criticized for not including personal attributes. Ennis defined the term as a "reasonable reflective thinking focused on deciding what to believe or do".

After studying all these definitions and comparing them to each other, we can say that there exists tremendous potential for conflict in defining an elusive term and a vague concept like critical thinking. The ambiguity of the concept arises mostly from the fact that most thinkers have tried to offer a concise definition of an otherwise long and intricate process. Instead of trying to encapsulate the while process in one or two lines, the thinkers should focus on each and every important component of critical thinking and incorporate it in their definition. To the sake of brevity, they should not include explanation of the components. One such definition was offered by Halpern (1996). Diane Halpern carefully takes into account every important component of the concept and includes them in her definition. According to her, critical thinking refers to "the use of those cognitive skills or strategies that increase the probability of a desirable outcome. It is used to describe thinking that is purposeful, reasoned and goal directed - the kind of thinking involved in solving problems, formulating inferences, calculating likelihood's, and making decisions when the thinker is using skills that are thoughtful and effective for the particular context and type of thinking task. Critical thinking also involves evaluating the thinking process - the reasoning that went into the conclusion we've arrived at the kinds of factors considered in making a decision. Critical thinking is sometimes called directed thinking because it focuses on a desired outcome."

Critical thinking is therefore not an easy process to define. However it is important to focus on each individual component of the concept and grasp it properly in order to understand critical thinking process on the whole. While there is no unanimously accepted definition of critical thinking, educators and researchers have agreed on some of the important components of the concept, which can help us develop the habit and ability of thinking critically. Critical thinking involves careful evaluation of information, serious and complete unbiased reflection, and it must be accompanied with a sincere desire to reach objective results. Objectivity is the most important mental attributes that one needs to develop or possess in order to become a critical thinker. Biased opinion and clouded thinking interfere with the process of critical thinking and for this reason emotions must not be allowed to affect one's ability to think critically.

Foot-Notes

Scriven, M., & Paul, R. (1992, November). Critical thinking defined. Handout given at Critical Thinking Conference, Atlanta, GA.
Chance, P. (1986). Thinking in the classroom: A survey of programs. New York: Teachers College, Columbia University
Ennis, R. (1992). Critical thinking: What is it? Proceedings of the Forty-Eighth Annual Meeting of the Philosophy of Education Society Denver, Colorado, March 27-30.
"The Delphi Report" By Dr. Peter A. Facione, Dean of the College of Arts and Sciences Santa Clara University 1990
Dewey, J. (1909) revised edition (1993). How we think: A restatement of the relation of reflective thinking to the educative process. Boston: Houghton Mifflin Company.
Halpern, Diane F. Thought and Knowledge: An Introduction to Critical Thinking. 1996.

Chapter 6

What's Critical About Critical Thinking?

Individuals and researchers should never underestimate the importance of critical thinking. Critical thinking affects each and every individual's life, as well as society in general, both in the short-term and long run. Examples of decisions involving critical thinking include economic choices, educational decisions, occupational choices, political decisions, religious choices, and social choices. What makes critical thinking so invaluable is that decisions made with little or no critical thinking frequently backfires, creating greater difficulties. In order to avoid potential difficulties and unexpected surprises, individuals and organizations must continually engage in critical thinking, adapting their ways as time and other factors dictate.

Decision-Making

It is interesting to note that while critical thinking must involve decision-making, decision-making does not have to involve critical thinking. For example, I can make any decision without thinking rationally about it. I can choose

to leave my job and move to Rome without critically assessing whether this is an appropriate decision. I can choose to accept that Nike must be a great shoe because Michael Jordan wears it and decide never to wear anything else. These are decisions but without being considered decisions, they are not critical thinking."
Decision-making is simply the steps taken to come to a conclusion, whether those steps are logical or not.

Interestingly, decision-making does not have to be an individual process. Decision-making can occur in groups as well. This is experienced daily in democracies or consensus settings. This pluralistic view of decision-making occurs in a variety of settings such as: governments, businesses, and families. The end result, however, is the same - an alternative is selected as the response to a situation."
The next few chapters analyze and examine the multitude of issues related to the importance of Critical thinking, presented in two distinct sections. Part I"Critical Thinking and Forces of Influence" and the last section Part II "Strategic Planning in the Non-Profit World".

Importance Of Critical Thinking

Critical thinking is important for numerous reasons. **First**, in order to select the best course of action among different options available, individuals and organizations need to weigh the advantages and disadvantages of each choice. By engaging in critical thinking early in a developmental process, individuals and organizations will be less likely to encounter unexpected difficulties and will be more likely to be prepared should trouble arise. Next, critical thinking enables groups and individuals to potentially view situations in new ways, perhaps discovering more efficient and stronger alternatives than those previously considered.
Foot-Notes

Facione, Peter. "Critical Thinking: What It Is and Why It Counts." Retrieved from http://www.calpress.com/pdf_files/what&why.pdf on June "2005".

Van Gelder, Tim. "Critical Thinking on the Web." Retrieved from http://www.philosophy.unimelb.edu.au/reason/critical/ on June "2005".

"Foundation for Critical Thinking." Retrieved from http://www.criticalthinking.org/ on June"2005".

Critical Thinking for Critical Times

Chapter 7

Elements Of Critical Thinking

There are several essential elements of critical thinking.
*First, individuals and organizations should identify the issue or problems that need to be addressed.
*Next, groups and individuals need to identify and outline all possible courses of action in response to the issue or problem.
*Third, individuals and organizations must outline and evaluate the various advantages and disadvantages associated with each potential option.
*Fourth, groups and individuals should weigh the severity and urgency of the issue or problem as well as the costs and benefits of the most desirable course of action.
*Fifth, individuals and organizations need to select one to two options and decide how and when to implement such alternatives in view of their needs.
*Sixth, upon the selection and implementation of the chosen options, groups and individuals must decide whether to alter their chosen alternatives, eliminate their course of action in favor of another, or to devise new solutions.

*Seventh, individuals and organizations must react to any unanticipated issues or problems that arise out of the implementation of their chosen course of action, and *Lastly, groups and individuals need to maintain sight of their original goals as well as their long-term goals and how to balance their needs with the available options.

Mental Modals for Guiding the Thinking process

Individuals use various tactics to guide their thinking process. **First**, groups and individuals base their thinking process on their long term and short term needs both practical as well as hopeful. Examples of practical objectives include financial issues (income and expenses), product related issues (i.e., new products, updating or eliminating old or unprofitable goods), personnel issues (i.e., are more or fewer employees needed, is management guiding the company properly), etc. **Second**, individuals and organizations use their personal beliefs (i.e., ethics, morals, religious principles) to guide their thinking process. By balancing practical goals as well as theoretical principles, groups and individuals will be in a better position to avoid unexpected pitfalls and further trouble. **Thirdly**, groups and organizations use trial and error in order to guide their thinking process, adapting their strategy as their current and future needs dictate.

Conclusion:

Few things in life are as invaluable as critical thinking. Not only does critical thinking affect individuals and organizations, but it also impacts society in general. Various factors involved in critical thinking include organization, logic, scientific thinking, persuasion, problem solving, evaluation, decision, and action. Each factor impacts the short term and long run goals and options available to groups and organizations. What are essential in critical thinking is the ability to remain flexible as well as the foresight to project the needs and objectives of individuals and organizations.

Foot-notes

Facione, Peter. *"Critical Thinking: What It Is and Why It Counts." Retrieved from http://www.calpress.com/pdf_files/what&why.pdf on June "2005".*

Van Gelder, Tim. *"Critical Thinking on the Web." Retrieved from http://www.philosophy.unimelb.edu.au/reason/critical/ on June "2005".*

"Foundation for Critical Thinking." Retrieved from http://www.criticalthinking.org/ on June"2005".

Critical Thinking for Critical Times

Chapter 8

Critical Thinking Skills

Critical thinking skills involve more than observing information as black and white. It is probing deeper below the obvious to discover the core of the problem or situation. Only then can a knowledgeable decision be made. Critical thinking skills are evidenced through a variety of thinking styles such as systematic, intuitive, and creative.

Systematic Decision making

Systematic decision makers "tend to take a more logical, structured, step-by-step approach to solving a problem". Karen Dillon notes in her article the eight steps of systematic decision-making:

Eight Steps in Systematic Decision-Making

1. Address the right decision problem.
2. Clarify your real objectives.
3. Develop a range of creative alternatives.
4. Understand the consequences of your decision.

Critical Thinking for Critical Times

5. Make appropriate trade-offs among conflicting objectives.
6. Deal sensibly with uncertainties.
7. Take account of your risk-taking attitude.
8. Plan ahead for decisions.

Similar to scientific and logical thinking styles, the systematic thinking style looks first at the 'real' problem. Managers must use their critical thinking skills to discount irrelevant information and find the actual problem before proceeding through the systematic problem solving steps.

Intuition

Intuition is another critical thinking style. Many of the decisions made using intuition are trial and error. Intuition usually contributes to decisions where risk and uncertainty are prevalent. Some people, like Edward de Bono, author of several books on the creative process, "see intuition as a set of mental tools separate from logic and judgment that an individual can develop through practice and training." Intuition is often referred to as a 'gut instinct' or 'sixth sense.' Intuition skills can be learned. It does involve staying close to the problem, listening to what is being said or not said, going with a hunch and following it through to the end. Intuition skills are becoming important abilities in today's decision-making world.

Creativity

Creativity, another critical thinking style, draws upon the inner person: "The ability to be "creative" has become a critical component of business acumen." Dr. Edward de Bono, a leading authority on creative and conceptual thinking developed, the Six Thinking Hats in the early 1980s. Dr. de Bono's imaginary hats allow managers and others to focus on a particular disposition when faced with a problem. Each hat represents a different way of thinking; a White Hat focuses on factual information, a Red Hat on emotional intuition, a Yellow Hat on positive perspective, a Black Hat on caution, a Green Hat on creativity and a Blue Hat on control, overview and organization. By 'trying on' the various hats, managers can get different perspectives on a particular problem. Using these perspectives, along with other information relating to the problem, a manager can make a sound decision.

Critical Thinking for Critical Times 35

Chapter 9

Influences On Critical Thinking

Critical thinking styles vary, as do the forces of influence upon managerial decisions. Influence is defined as "a behavioral response to the exercise of power". It is a process of doing or saying something to get someone to choose this decision over that decision. This influence can come through such forces as ethics, gender and economic status.

Ethics

What is ethics and how can it influence thinking and decision-making? Webster defines ethics as "the system or code of morals of a particular person, religion, group, profession, etc." Ethics in the business world is very important. Everybody's perception is different; everyone else does not always view the right decision as the right decision. Doctors promise to uphold a certain ethical standard when they take the Hippocratic Oath. Not all professions have such a document; therefore, people must rely on what they believe or have been taught to be right or wrong. A manager must be able to realize the positive and

Critical Thinking for Critical Times   37

negative influences in regards to ethical behavior and decision-making. Using good ethical standards, a manager can put aside any personal goals or biases and concentrate on the information available.

Gender

Gender can also influence thinking and decision-making. Men no longer dominate the work/labor forces. Women are making their presence known, serving in administrative positions, CEO's and even business owners. *Gender* can play a role in personnel hiring practices, wage earnings and promotions. A good manager will look at the qualifications of the applicant and his OR her potential in regards to the position. Some occupations will always be gender biased, but change is the only constant in life so anything is possible. Managers need to realize the influencing powers of gender as well. Permitting certain behaviors with one gender while disciplining that same behavior with another gender will not help a manager gain respect from his/her subordinates. He/She must be able to overlook such influences and look at the facts of the situation before him.

Economical Status

Another influential force to be reckoned with is that of economic status. Affluent neighborhoods and powerful businessmen can use their financial security to persuade decisions in their favor, while less fortunate areas suffer. An effective manager will recognize this force and along with good ethical standards, will be able to make a decision based upon what is in the best interest of the person(s) or groups involved.

Conclusion:

Critical thinking styles and forces of influence play major roles in the decision-making process. An effective manager will use his/her skills to evaluate the problem or situation, push aside biases and influences and make a well-informed decision. There are no guarantees that a particular decision will be the 'right' choice; however, through critically thinking skills, the chances are better that the decision will be more 'right' than 'wrong.'

Critical Thinking for Critical Times

Chapter 10

Challenges Faced By Non-Profit Organizations

The major challenge faced today by the non-profit organizations is that of "devolution". The term of "Devolution" is used by the non-profit professionals to describe the cutbacks in the federal funding for non-profit organizations. Recent laws passed by Congress have reduced the obligations of the federal government in providing assistance to the needy and the poor. Federal government has adopted a new strategy for the distribution of grants and funds for several social programs. According to this new arrangement, funds will be assigned to states, allowing them to allocate these funds as the states see fit. Although, with the decentralization of funding operations, there should be lesser bureaucratic red tape and more control at the local level but the services programs initiated by the non-profit organizations will be exposed to a greater level of risk because of reduced federal funding. Due to the absence of federal contributions, most of the non-profit organizations will be facing significant financial problems because they receive around 30 to 40 percent of their funding from federal sources. To worsen the situation, these organizations are faced with a continuous increase in demand for human services. Services will be very difficult to fulfill under this current scenario.

Devolution has created several challenges for the leaders of non-profit organizations. Administrators will have to run their functions with greater efficiency, but with a reduced level of resources. In this regard, they have to redefine their operating procedures and try to search for other sources of funding. With the lack of funds for human services, non-profit organizations will have to adopt several traditional "for profit" organizational strategies like strategic alliances and restructuring. ***

Fundraising and Fees

Another challenge faced by the non-profit organizations is of fees and fundraising. Fees are usually charged by these organizations for the services provided by them and are to be paid by either the person receiving it or a third party such as the government or any other charity organization. However, a fee is not the primary source of revenue for non-profit organizations because their fees rarely cover the cost of the product or service being provided. This is the reason why non-profit organizations search extensively for additional revenue sources and get involved in different fund raising activities.

Interestingly, the services provided by the non-profit organizations are of high worth to the communities but it is extremely difficult to measure the outcomes of these services. It may take years to experience a significant change in the behavior of the society because of the efforts of any organization. As a result of this limitation, non-profit organizations are unable to demonstrate results of their efforts and therefore donors become hesitant to make their contributions. This limits their sources of funding.

As mentioned earlier, leaders of non-profit organizations have to extensively rely on external sources of funding to meet the demand for human services. They must get engaged in fundraising activities. Fundraising, however, this is not a very pleasant job. It requires considerable effort on the part of the top management of the organization. They have to dedicate sufficient amount of time to fundraising activities, which makes it very difficult for them to keep a balance between fundraising activities and other organizational assignments.

Non-profit organizations seek funding from several sources. The primary source is grants awarded by the government, charitable foundations, or for-profit corporations, to support specific social development programs. Although, grants provided by the government are based on a rough estimate of the cost of services provided by a particular agency but funding awarded by corporations are to be used with caution as the organization has to submit a report on the program's activities and expenses incurred during the program. In addition to these major sources of funds, non-profit organizations contact individuals as well for donations.

These donations are collected either through establishing close relationship with the community members or by asking individuals to become a member of the organization. Although donations are often small in volume, if they come from a large number of people, this may become a significant source of funds. There are individuals who make sizable contributions and are referred to as "major" donors. Organizations usually allocate substantial time and energy to attract such major donors. Several special events are also organized by these organizations to raise funds.

A successful Major Gifts fund-raising campaign is not magic. It is a straightforward, concise process of executing well-defined components arranged in a step-by-step progression. To that end, I suggest that the checklist below be used to self-evaluate your organization's Major Gifts fund-raising readiness at a special board meeting, at a staff retreat, or as a one-on-one survey of trustees and staff.

Major Gifts Fund-Raising Program:

29 Step Checklists for Major Fund- Raising Works from a General Development Plan

- Operates with other campaigns without diluting any of our resources
- Has a solid base of major gifts from our Board of Trustees
- Functions with the guidance of a Development Committee of the Board
- Has the staff in place to provide all of the needed campaign resources
- Involves and informs our organization's other departments and personnel
- Prioritizes individuals, corporations, foundations for maximum potential
- Rates and evaluates prospects for their maximum giving potential
- Provides suggested asking amounts to all prospects
- Features challenge and matching gifts to attract the gifts of others
- Always settles upon achievable goals before we start to solicit
- Presents a compelling case for support
- Maintains stewardship and cultivation programs for donors and prospects
- Projects what numbers of gifts in what amounts we need to meet goals
- Promotes gifts via memberships and other named opportunities
- Develops campaign time-lines for the leadership and solicitors
- Provides job descriptions and duties for the leadership and solicitors
- Equips our solicitation team with the best information and instruction

- Provides solicitation training with special focus upon the asking process
- Features one-on-one and partners for the actual asking of gifts
- Seeks to have the best possible prospect to solicitor assignments
- Benefits from a full range of relevant publicity and promotion activities
- Provides progress reports and other regular campaign updates
- Ensures that all requests for contributions are followed to completion
- Obtains in all instances, reasons individuals refused or reduced their gifts
- Records gifts and collects the money in a timely fashion
- Promptly acknowledges donors' gifts and apprises the respective solicitors
- Announces results, gives recognition and thanks donors and volunteers
- Reviews and assesses all completed campaigns to improve the next ones

Fundraising becomes a full time job and may distract the attention of organization's leaders from other important activities such as organizing and managing. If the leaders will get increasingly involved in fundraising activities, devoting lesser time to operational tasks of the organization, their subordinates will loose direction. This will in turn negatively affect the performance of the organization and will limit its ability to effectively make positive contributions to society. To increase the efficiency of the fundraising efforts non-profit organizations should strive to bring improvements in their programs. In addition to this, the leadership of the organization should be committed to achieve its goals or objectives.

Recruiting & orienting quality of service:

In non-profit organizations, providing high quality services is a major challenge. With limited resources and lack of well-trained staff, it becomes nearly impossible for them to provide the quality of service at the desired levels. The primary reasons for lower quality of service are limited resources and lower level of performance by employees. As discussed before, it is very difficult for the non-profit organizations to attract and retain well-trained and qualified employees. Therefore their workforce is often not capable of providing the best possible service.

In addition to this, increasing demands for human services have forced these organizations to devote more time and resources in providing service, which, in turn, has forced the employees to devote more time and energy to their jobs. As a result of the increasing work pressure, the quality of service often starts to decline.

Another reason, which causes the quality of services provided by the non-profit organizations to decline, is the extra focus of the leaders of these organizations on issues of fund raising and finances. As these leaders are unable to devote their full attention on other important issues, the performance of their teams starts to decline.

The solution to the problem of lower quality service is that these organizations should continuously invest some money on the training of their staff.

Moreover, in order to reduce the work pressure, they should encourage that volunteers participate in their different social services programs.

The leaders of these organizations should also keep a balance between their assignments and should devote enough time for monitoring and controlling the operations of the organization. These actions will help organizations retain high quality personnel.

Some other challenges faced by non-profit organizations include lack of sufficient resources to compensate the leadership, lack of managerial training and inability to seek outside advice or consultation. Lack of funds limits the ability of the non-profit organizations to attract, retain and compensate good managers, which creates several administrative problems. As the career in non-profit organizations requires hard work and offers little opportunities for career advancement, few of the talented individuals stay in this profession for long. This is the reason why non-profit organizations lack managerial expertise and training. Majority of the individuals working in non-profit organizations are from non-management discipline and therefore do not have the necessary skills that are required to run a non-profit organizations. Another problem is that majority of the non-profit organizations are hesitant to spend money on hiring outside management consultants, because of the lack of funds.

Conclusion

To overcome these obstacles, leaderships of non-profit organizations should take measures to resolve the problem. To attract talented individuals, these organizations should offer some additional perks, if they cannot offer high compensations. Moreover, they should spend some money in training their staff so that their resources could be effectively managed and programs could be managed effectively. Outside consultants should also be hired so that internal problems of the organization could be identified. Even if any organization cannot afford to hire outside consultants, some low cost volunteer assistance can also be helpful.

Critical Thinking for Critical Times

Chapter 11

Strategic Planning In The Non-profit Sector

Strategic management is defined as "the set of decisions and actions used to formulate and implement strategies that will provide a competitively superior fit between the organization and its environment so as to achieve organizational objectives". This definition applies equally to profit and non-profit companies. Both types are required being competitive. For example, the non-profit company must be competitive in attracting the resources it requires to achieve its goals. While this basic definition applies to both, the non-profit organization does have some special aspect that impacts on its strategic planning process. Crittenden & Crittenden offers a thorough analysis of strategic planning for non-profits:

Aspects of the strategic planning process have increased importance for the non-profit sector. Specifically, certain elements that are minor considerations in the profit sector are key considerations in the non-profit sector. These elements include:

Critical Thinking for Critical Times 49

1. Administrative style; 2. Membership involvement; 3.strategic planning routines; 4.subjective planning; and 5.resource misallocation.

As differing from profit organizations, non-profit organizations can be divided into two general types: *instrumental* and *expressive*.

Instrumental non-profit organizations are focused on some issue that is not specific to its members. **Expressive organizations** are those where the activities of members are carried out to help the members. The focus of each is very different. For the instrumental the focus is outside the group. For the expressive the focus is inside the group. This explains why the planning would differ between the two. Instrumental groups by their very nature have some external long-term goal to accomplish. Therefore, it is logical that they would be more mission-based. In contrast, the expressive group is less likely to feel the need for long-term plans since its members are working towards the same thing.

In addition to this, it is noted that non-profit organizations often exhibit inward-looking and outward-looking tendencies at the same time. This seems to be something that is necessary for the non-profit organization that requires its support from outside sources. Expressive organizations may be focused inwards but they also need to focus outwards to concentrate on attracting the membership that allows them to exist. Similarly, instrumental groups need to look outward to attract the funding and membership they need.

This leads to the next important point, which is that the non-profit organization has a greater link with the external environment. A profit organization is actually more self-contained in this way. They may need to sell product to achieve their goals but this can be done with a minor focus on the external environment to determine what product to provide and then a major focus on the internal environment

50 Ronald E. White, Sr.

to determine how to provide it. The non-profit organization is different in that its major focus must be the external environment.

Resource misallocation

One type of organization is described as having a large proportion of type "A" members and an type "A" administrator with little managerial experience. This organization shows a significant lack of control, having a lot of planners but not an adequate plan and a tendency to misallocate resources. This is a case where all members of the organization are there for the same reason, yet the purpose neither is nor defined. This shows the importance of providing adequate leadership. Even if the goals are internal and based on the members, the organization could benefit from leadership that recognizes the purpose and allocates resources effectively. It seems that without a clear leader and a clear mission, time and money is wasted. Even if the goal of a non-profit organization is simply a social one, effective management is still beneficial to members.

Consider the example of a book club. This book club may exist primarily as a means of socializing, with this the basic desire of all members. Planning based on this mission could help all members. For example, membership fees could be used to pay for group outings or the purchase of books. This illustrates that effective planning and management should not only be a priority of non-profit groups with a serious objective.

The difference that age makes to a group is also noted, with younger members joining organizations for the social factors while older members tend to join instrumental groups. In most non-profit organizations, it is important to attract a diverse range of members. For example, if an instrumental group has only older members, it may lose touch with younger society, not attract future members and begin to shrink in size. Looked at from the opposite perspective, an expressive group may also miss out on the experience older members have to offer. In addition, it is likely that older members are the ones with the finances to support a group. Therefore, all groups may need to consider what kind of membership they are attracting and alter their focus to attract a new kind of member.

The final important point made is that non-profit organizations tend to focus on one funding source instead of drawing their funds from various areas. This may be an issue of concern if that source of funding becomes limited. If this happens, the organization may find itself in a difficult position. This is an area where ongoing planning may be required. The fact that many organizations source their funds from one area raises the questions of whether non-profit organizations pay enough attention to this area. An organization in the profit sector is always focused on where funding comes from since profit is their basic reason for existence. In the non-profit sector, some other goal is the focus. However, while the other goal is the organization's reason for existing, generating revenue is still a requirement. As one source notes, "as with any business firm, a non-profit organization needs resources and support to survive and achieve its objectives." The challenge for the non-profit organization is to manage two sets of goals simultaneously, the *first* to generate income and the *second*, to use it as effectively as possible to achieve its major goal.

Conclusion

Overall, this chapter, and the book as a whole illustrates several areas that are of specific importance to the non-profit organization. Clearly, the non-profit organization operates differently than the profit organization and so its strategic planning and critical thinking skills must exceed the challenges of the critical times in which we live.

Critical Thinking for Critical Times

References

Facione, Peter. "Critical Thinking: What It Is and Why It Counts." Retrieved from http://www.calpress.com/pdf_files/what&why.pdf on June "2005".

Van Gelder, Tim. "Critical Thinking on the Web." Retrieved from: http://www.philosophy.unimelb.edu.au/reason/critical/ on June "2005".

"Foundation for Critical Thinking." Retrieved from http://www.criticalthinking.org/ on June "2005".

Agnes, M. (Ed.). (1999). Webster's new world college dictionary. New York: Macmillan

Dessler, G. (1998). Management: leading people and organizations in the 21st century. NJ: Prentice Hall, Inc.

Dillon, K. (1998, October). The perfect decision. Inc. Vol 20, Iss 14, p. 74.

Jennings, L. (1999, March). Intuition in Decision-Making. Futurist. Vol 33, Iss 3, p. 44.

Schermerhorn, J., Hunt, J., & Osborn. R. (2000). Organizational Behavior. (7th ed). New York: John Wiley & Sons, Inc.

Thompson, P. & Brooks, K. (1997, July/August). A creative approach to strategic planning. CMA Magazine.

What color is your hat? (1994, September). Executive Report. Vol 13, Iss 1, p. 6.

Kent E. Dove: Conducting a Successful Capital Campaign: The New, Revised and Expanded Edition of the Leading Guide to

Critical Thinking for Critical Times

Planning and Implementing a Capital Campaign: Jossey-Bass: 2nd edition: October 1999

Stanley Weinstein & Robert F. Hartsook: The Complete Guide to Fund-Raising Management: John Wiley & Sons: 2nd edition: February 2002

Michael Allison & Jude Kaye: Strategic Planning for Non-profit Organizations: A Practical Guide and Workbook: John Wiley & Sons: July 1997

Crittenden, W.F., & Crittenden, V.L. "Relationships between organizational characteristics and strategic planning processes in non-profit organizations."

Journal of Managerial Issues 12:2 (Summer 2000): 150-168.
Daft, R.L. Management. Fort Worth, TX: The Dryden Press, 1997.
Perreault, W.D., & McCarthy, E.J. Essentials of Marketing. Boston: Irwin, 2000.

Alliance (2004). FAQ. Alliance for Risk Management. http://www.allianceon line.org/FAQ/risk_management/what_are_most_common_1.faq

Analysis of FASB 117. (2003). The Non Profit Resource Center. http://www.1800net.com/nprc/fasb117.html

Dennis, A. (1997). Managing with a mission. Journal of Accountancy, 184(4): 71-75.

Fee, D. (2000). Understanding financial operations. Association Management, 52(1): 112-114

Goehner, D. (1999). Protecting your organization against financial misuse. Non-profit World, 17(4): 38-39.

Langan, J.P. (1998). Understanding non-profit financial management. Association Management, 50(1): 75.

Little, H.B. (2001). Analyze your finances to ensure your mission. Non-profit World, 19(5): 31-33.

Ruiz, R. (1999). Are you fulfilling your financial trust? Non-profit World, 17(1): 22-

Stout, W. (2001). Measure your use of time. Non-profit World, 19(4): 28-33.

Umapathy, S. (1993). Financial risk management: the board's responsibility. Non-profit World, 11(5): 10-14.

Young, D. R. (1999). Economic decisionmaking by non-profit organizations in a market economy: tensions between mission and market. Case Western Reserve University. Paper presented to the independent sector spring research forum. The National Center on Non-profit Enterprise. http://www.nationalcne.org/papers/tension.htm

Critical Thinking for Critical Times

Glossary

Non-Profit and For-Profit terminology

501(c)(3): Section of the Internal Revenue Code that designates an organization as charitable, tax-exempt, and non-profit. Organizations qualifying under the Code include religious, educational, charitable, amateur athletic, scientific or literacy groups. AWS is a 501(c)(3) organization.

509(a): Section of the Code that defines public charities, as opposed to private foundations. A 501(c)(3) organization may also have a 509(a) designation to further define the agency as a public charity.

990: The tax information form filed annually with IRS and the state's Attorney General's office by all tax-exempt organizations.

A

Abstract: A short summary of a project or program including all pertinent aspects of the sponsored activity, a summary of the objectives and expected results. The abstract is usually less than 350 words and limited to one double spaced typed page.

Amount: Amount purchased or sold in Gift Fund Pools as a result of a contribution or miscellaneous activity.

Annual Report: A voluntary report published by a foundation or corporation describing its grant activities. A

Critical Thinking for Critical Times 59

growing number of foundations and corporations use annual reports to inform the community about their contributions, activities, policies, and guidelines.
Assets: The amount of capital or principal — money, stocks, bonds, real estate, or other resources — controlled by a foundation or corporate giving program. Generally, assets are invested and the resulting income is used to make grants.

Articles of Incorporation
A legal document that creates specific type of organization, a corporation, under the laws of a particular state. State law prescribes specific statements that must be included in Articles of Incorporation, and non-profit corporations in particular
must include certain provisions in order to qualify as non-profit under state law. Furthermore, in order to obtain federal tax-exempt status, certain provisions must be included either in a non-profit organization's Articles of Incorporation or its Bylaws.

B

Back-End Premium
A term used to describe a (generally) low cost item that is sent by charitable soliciting organizations to donors as a modest form of thanks. See also front-end premium.

Beneficiary: In philanthropic terms, the donee or grantee receiving funds from a foundation or corporate giving program is the beneficiary, although society benefits as well.

Bequest: A sum of money or other property available upon the donor's death.

Board of Directors

See Board of Trustees.
Board of Trustees
Also termed the "Board of Directors." In a non-profit corporation, the Board of Trustees represents the interests of the general public or the specific public group that the organization was established to serve.

Building Campaign: A drive to raise funds for construction or renovation of buildings.

Business An organization established for generating profit. A commercial organization

Bylaws
A legal document stating certain self-imposed rules adopted for the regulation of an organization's own actions. Since it is a required element when forming a corporation, Bylaws are a form of agreement or contract between the corporation and its owners to conduct itself in a certain way. While for a commercial business the owners are its shareholders, the ownership of a non-profit corporation belongs to the public as represented by the NPO's Board of Trustees and the government

C

Capital Grant: Grant to provide funding for buildings, construction, or equipment, rather than program or operating expenses.

Capital Campaign: An organized drive to raise substantial funds to finance major needs of an organization, including construction, renovations, or endowment.

Capital support: Funds provided for endowment purposes, buildings, construction, or equipment, and including, for example, grants for "bricks and mortar."

Case law
The body of written law established through judicial decisions, instead of legislative action (which establishes statutory law).

Certificate of Authority
A license issued by a state's Secretary of State giving permission for a foreign corporation to operate in that state. This license is required before operating a business establishment or otherwise engaging in commerce in that state, such as hiring that state's residents as employees. However, some activities that are conducted in a state by a commercial or non-profit organization may not constitute sufficient presence (called "nexus") in that state to require a Certificate of Authority.

Challenge Grant: A grant that is made on the condition that other funding is secured, either on a matching basis or by some other formula, usually within a specified period of time, with the objective of encouraging expanded fundraising from additional sources.

Charitable organization
In the Model Solicitations Act (1986), "Charitable organization" means:
"(1) Any person determined by the Internal Revenue Service to be a tax exempt organization pursuant to section 501(c)(3) of the Internal Revenue Code; or
(2) Any person who is or holds himself out to be established for any benevolent, educational, philanthropic, humane, scientific, patriotic, social welfare or advocacy, public health, environmental conservation, civic or other eleemosynary purpose or for the benefit of law enforcement personnel, firefighters, or other persons who protect the public safety, or any person who in any manner employs a charitable appeal as the basis of any solicitation or an

appeal which has a tendency to suggest there is a charitable purpose to any such solicitation."

Charitable purpose
In the Model Solicitations Act (1986), "charitable purpose" means:
Any purpose described in Internal Revenue Code section 501(c)(3); or
(2) Any benevolent, educational, philanthropic, humane, scientific, patriotic, social welfare or advocacy, public health, environmental conservation, civic or other eleemosynary objective, or an objective that benefits law enforcement personnel, firefighters, or other persons who protect the public safety."

Charitable sales promotion
In the Model Solicitations Act (1986), "charitable sales promotion" means "an advertising or sales campaign, conducted by a commercial co-venturer, which represents that the purchase or use of goods or services offered by the commercial co-venturer will benefit, in whole or in part, a charitable organization or purpose."

Charitable solicitation
See solicitation.

Charity, Charitable
Some common meanings of "charity" are, (1) benevolent goodwill toward or love of humanity, (2) lenient judgment of others, (3) generosity and helpfulness especially toward the needy or suffering; also aid given to those in need, (4) public provision for the relief of the needy, (5) an institution engaged in relief of the poor, (6) a gift for public benevolent purposes, or an institution founded by such a gift. See also charitable organization and charitable purpose.

Critical Thinking for Critical Times   63

Commercial, Commerce, Commodity

Occupied with or engaged in commerce or work intended for commerce. Commerce is the exchange, buying, or selling of commodities. A commodity is an economic good, or something useful or valued. However, when used in law with regard to non-profit organizations, "commerce" is specifically considered to be engaged in for the purpose of creating profit.

Commercial organization

See business.

Commercial co-venturer, coventurer

In the Model Solicitations Act (1986) "commercial co-venturer" means a "person who for profit is regularly and primarily engaged in trade or commerce other than in connection with soliciting for charitable organizations or purposes and who conducts a charitable sales promotion." Sometimes a law will simply refer to a "coventurer" with the same meaning.

A compilation of state definitions of the term "commercial co- venturer" and related terms is available at this site

Committed Funds : The portion of a donor's budget that has already been pledged for future allocation.

Common law

Unwritten law primarily based on custom, but also sometimes referring to a system of law originating in England.

Community foundation: A 501(c)(3) organization that makes grants for charitable purposes in a specific community or region. The funds available to a community foundation are usually derived from many donors and held in an endowment that is independently administered; income earned by the endowment is then used to make

64 *Ronald E. White, Sr.*

grants. Although a community foundation may be classified by the IRS as a private foundation, most are classified as public charities and are thus eligible for maximum tax-deductible contributions from the general public. See also 501(c)(3); public charity.

Community fund: An organized community program which makes annual appeals to the general public for funds that are usually not retained in an endowment but are instead used for the ongoing operational support of local agencies. See also federated giving program

Company-sponsored foundation (also referred to as a corporate foundation): A private foundation whose assets are derived primarily from the contributions of a for-profit business. While a company-sponsored foundation may maintain close ties with its parent company, it is an independent organization with its own endowment and as such is subject to the same rules and regulations as other private foundations. See also private foundation.

Compensation
Something that constitutes an equivalent or recompense. A reward for services rendered. Compensation may be monetary (in cash or cash equivalents) or non-monetary (in property or intangible benefits). Also see consideration.

Consideration
The inducement, price or motive that causes a party to enter into an agreement or contract. Also see compensation.

Contribution
In the Model Solicitations Act (1986), "contribution" means "the grant, promise or pledge of money, credit, property, financial assistance or other thing of any kind or value in response to a solicitation. It does not include bona fide fees, dues or assessments paid by members, provided

Critical Thinking for Critical Times 65

that membership is not conferred solely as consideration for making a contribution in response to a solicitation."

Cooperating Collection: A member of the Foundation Center's network of libraries, community foundations, and other non-profit agencies that provides a core collection of Center publications in addition to a variety of supplementary materials and services in areas useful to grant-seekers.

Cooperative venture: A joint effort between or among two or more grant-makers. Cooperative venture partners may share in funding responsibilities or contribute information and technical resources.

Corporation
A form of legal entity created under state law. This entity is treated much like an individual under law, and therefore the term "person" in law usually means both individuals and corporations. Their Articles of Incorporation and Bylaws govern corporations.

Corporate Contributions: General term referring to charitable contributions by a corporation. Usually used to describe cash contributions only, but may also include other items, such as the value of loaned executives, products, and services.

Corporate Foundation: A foundation that receives its income from a profit-making company but is a legally independent entity. Usually this type of foundation carries the name of the parent company. Corporations may fund these foundations with a donation of permanent assets or with periodic contributions.

Corporate Giving Program: Funding distributed directly by a corporation rate Giving Program rather than through a foundation.

Counsel
An advisor, often a legal or financial advisor. A counsel does not usually perform the actions that are advised himself or herself, which are instead performed by the person or organization that the advisor serves. See also fundraising counsel

D

Declining Grant: A multi-year grant that becomes smaller each year, in the expectation that the recipient organization will increase its fundraising from other sources.

Demonstration Grant: A grant made to establish an innovative project or program which, if successful, will serve as a model and may be duplicated by others.

Discretionary Funds: Grant monies which are distributed according to a donor's judgment of requests as they are received, rather than funds whose purpose is predetermined.

DIALOG: An online database information service made available by Knight Ridder Information Services, Inc. The Foundation Center offers two large files on foundations and grants through DIALOG.

Direct Costs: Includes all items that can be categorically identified and charged to the specific project, such as personnel, fringe benefits, consultants, subcontractors, travel, equipment, supplies and materials, communications, computer time, and publication charges.

Critical Thinking for Critical Times 67

Distribution committee: The committee responsible for making grant decisions. For community foundations, the distribution committee is intended to be broadly representative of the community served by the foundation.

Domestic corporation
A corporation that was established in the jurisdiction being considered. For instance, a non-profit corporation incorporated in New York is a domestic corporation with respect to New York state laws. However, it is a foreign corporation with respect to the laws of every other state.

Donation
See contribution

Donee: Individual or organization that receives a grant. Also called a grantee.

Donor: Individual or organization that makes a grant. Also called a grantor.

E

Employee matching grant: A contribution to a charitable organization by an employee that is matched by a similar contribution from his or her employer. Many corporations have employee matching-gift programs in higher education that encourage their employees to give to the college or university of their choice.

Endowment: A bequest or gift that is intended to be kept permanently and invested in order to generate income for an organization or foundation.

Expenditure responsibility: In general, when a private foundation makes a grant to an organization that is not classified by the IRS as a "public charity," the foundation is required by law to provide some assurance that the funds will be used for the intended charitable purposes. Special reports on such grants must be filed with the IRS. Most grantee organizations are public charities and many foundations do not make "expenditure responsibility" grants.

F

Family Foundation: A private foundation created to make charitable contributions on behalf of a particular family. The board is often limited to family members.

Federated Fund Drive: A centralized campaign whereby one organization raises money for its member agencies. The United Way campaign is an example of a federated fund drive.

Federated giving program: A joint fundraising effort usually administered by a non-profit "umbrella" organization that in turn distributes the contributed funds to several non-profit agencies. United Way and community chests or funds, the United Jewish Appeal and other religious appeals, the United Negro College Fund, and joint arts councils are examples of federated giving programs. See also community fund.

Field offices: The Washington, D.C., Atlanta, Cleveland, and San Francisco reference collections operated by the Foundation Center, all of which offer a wide variety of services and comprehensive collections of information on foundations and grants

Foreign corporation
A corporation that was established outside of the jurisdiction under consideration. For instance, a non-profit organization incorporated in New York is a foreign

corporation with respect to Ohio state law, but is a domestic corporation with respect to New York law.

Foundation: A private non-profit organization with funds and a program managed by its own trustees and directors, established to further social, educational, religious or other charitable activities by making grants. A private foundation receives its funds from, and is subject to control of, an individual family, corporation or other group of limited number. In contrast, a community foundation receives its funds from multiple public sources and is classified by the IRS as a public charity.

Fundraising consultant
In the North Carolina General Statutes Section 131F-2(10), "fund-raising consultant" means "any person who meets all of the following:
a. Is retained by a charitable organization or sponsor for a fixed fee or rate under a written agreement to plan, manage, conduct, consult, or prepare material for the solicitation of contributions in this State.
b. Does not solicit contributions or employ, procure, or engage any person to solicit contributions.
c. Does not at any time have custody or control of contributions."
A key component of this definition is item (c), which distinguishes it from the definition of "fundraising counsel" given in the Model Solicitations Act (1986), as a person who does not solicit contributions but may have custody or control of the contributions at some point. Typically, the regulatory burden is less for a person who doesn't ever have custody or control of contributions. A person who either conducts the solicitation or has custody or control of contributions at any time is typically defined as a professional solicitor rather than a fundraising consultant.

70 — Ronald E. White, Sr.

Fundraising counsel
In the Model Solicitations Act (1986), "Fund raising counsel" means a "person who for compensation plans, manages, advises, consults, or prepares material for, or with respect to, the solicitation in this state of contributions for a charitable organization, but who does not solicit contributions and who does not employ, procure, or engage any compensated person to solicit contributions. No lawyer, investment counselor or banker who advises a person to make a contribution shall be deemed, as a result of such advice, to be a fund raising counsel. A bona fide salaried officer, employee or volunteer of a charitable organization shall not be deemed to be a fund raising counsel." Typically, the regulatory burden is less for a person who doesn't actually conduct the solicitation but only advises the non-profit organization. Note, however, that the Model Solicitations Act (1986) did not specify that a fundraising counsel never has custody or control of the contributions. Accordingly, some states have added such a requirement to their definition of this role, sometimes renaming it to fundraising consultant.

G

General/operating support: A grant made to further the general purpose or work of an organization, rather than for a specific purpose or project; also called an unrestricted grant.

General purpose foundation: An independent private foundation that awards grants in many different fields of interest. See also special purpose foundation.

Grantee financial report: A report detailing how grant funds were used by an organization. Many corporate grant makers require this kind of report from grantees. A financial report generally includes a listing of all expenditures from grant funds as well as an overall

Critical Thinking for Critical Times   71

organizational financial report covering revenue and expenses, assets and liabilities.

Grassroots fundraising: Efforts to raise money from individuals or groups from the local community on a broad basis. Usually an organization's own constituents — people who live in the neighborhood served or clients of the agency's services — are the sources of these funds. Grassroots fundraising activities include membership drives, raffles, auctions, benefits, and a range of other activities.

Guidelines: Procedures set forth by a funder that grantseekers should follow when approaching a grantmaker.

Grant: The award of funds to an organization or individual to undertake charitable or tax-exempt activities.

Grantee: Individual or organization that receives a grant. Also called a donee.

Grantor: Individual or organization that makes a grant. Also called a donor.

H

I

In-kind Contribution: Support in the form of goods or services rather than a cash contribution.

Independent Foundation: A private foundation that is no longer controlled by the original donor or donor's family.

Internal Revenue Code: The laws governing taxation in the United States, administered by the Internal Revenue Service.

Internal Revenue Service (IRS): The federal agency with responsibility for regulating public charities and foundations, as part of its authority under the Internal Revenue Code.

IRB: (Institutional Review Board) A ten member body which reviews, approves or disapproves any research involving human subjects.

J

Joint Funding: A Grant project supported by more than one donor, each of whom may provide monies for a specific component of the overall project or who may contribute to a common pool of funds.

Jurisdiction
The authority of a sovereign power to govern or legislate. The power or right to exercise authority. The limits or territory within which authority may be exercised.

K

L

M

Matching Gifts Program: A corporate contributions program that will match contributions made by employees, retirees, and their spouses to qualifying non-profit organizations. Each corporation establishes specific guidelines regarding the type of organizations included,

Critical Thinking for Critical Times 73

donor eligibility, and the dollar amount that will be matched.

Matching Grant: A grant or gift made with the specification that the amount donated must be matched from other sources on a one-for-one or some other prescribed basis.

Model Solicitations Act (1986)
A model law developed by the National Association of Attorneys General, the National Association of State Charity Officials, and the Private Sector Advisory Group and completed in 1986. The full title of the document is "A Model Act Concerning the Solicitation of Funds for Charitable Purposes." The Model Act was subsequently adopted by many states, but some portions were later ruled unconstitutional by the Supreme Court. A complete copy of the Model Act is available online.

N
_____

National Association of Attorneys General,
The National Association of Attorneys General (NAAG) was founded to facilitate interaction among Attorneys General as peers, and to facilitate the enhanced performance of Attorneys General and their staffs. The Association's 56 members are the Attorneys General of the 50 states and the chief legal officers of the District of Columbia (Corporation Counsel), the Commonwealths of Puerto Rico (Secretary of Justice) and the Northern Mariana Islands, and the territories of American Samoa, Guam, and the Virgin Islands. The U.S. Attorney General is an honorary member. This organization maintains a Web site.

Nexus
The condition of having sufficient presence in a jurisdiction to be subject to specific laws of that jurisdiction. For instance, in order to be subject to the taxing authority of a state, a person or organization must have sufficient presence in that state, usually established by operating a business or otherwise engaging in commerce there. The degree of presence and the associated specific conditions necessary for a nexus to be formed is typically established by statutory and case law.

Non-profit: A term describing the Internal Revenue Service's designation of an organization whose income is not used for the benefit or private gain of stockholders, directors, or any other persons with an interest in the company. A non-profit organization's income must be used solely to support its operations and stated purpose.

Non-profit organization, Non-profit corporation, NPO
An organization in which no owner, stockholder or trustee shares in profits and losses, and which exists not to earn revenue but to promote a mission that typically (but not necessarily) enhances the public welfare. These organizations are often eligible for tax-exempt status, but not all non-profit organizations are tax-exempt, nor can contributions to all non-profit organizations be treated as deductions for income tax purposes.

O

Operating foundation: A 501(c)(3) organization classified by the IRS as a private foundation whose primary purpose is to conduct research, social welfare, or other programs determined by its governing body or establishment charter. An operating foundation may make grants, but the sum generally is small relative to the funds used for the foundation's own programs. See also 501(c)(3).

Critical Thinking for Critical Times 75

Operating Support: Contributions toward an organization's day-to-day, ongoing expenses, such as salaries, utilities, office supplies, etc

P

Paid solicitor
See professional solicitor.

PDF-format
An electronic file format that represents text and graphical material independent of the particular display system, presenting a layout and style identical or nearly identical to the corresponding printed paper version. PDF-format is the format most commonly used by the IRS to publish forms online. PDF-format can be used either to display pages by constructing them from their component parts (i.e. text, lines, images, etc), or by simply presenting the scanned image of that page. The former method is much more compact and may be used with automated text searching mechanisms, but is much more labor intensive to create if starting from a printed page. PDF-format contrasts with HTML-format, which may be presented differently depending on the display mechanism. Another key difference is that while fill-out forms may be composed in PDF-format, online software that can process completed forms in this format are neither common nor inexpensive. PDF-format has been deemed acceptable in proposed IRS regulations for Internet publication of tax-returns and Applications for Exemption for tax-exempt organizations. **Payout Requirement:** Private foundations are required by law to pay out at least five percent of the fair market value of their assets each year in grants and administrative expenses.

Person
In legal meaning, a "person" may be an individual, a corporation, or some other entity created according to law. The Model Solicitations Act (1986), defines "person" as "an individual, corporation, association, partnership, trust, foundation or any other entity however styled."

Professional solicitor
Also termed a "paid solicitor" or sometimes just "solicitor." A professional solicitor is distinguished from a fundraising consultant or fundraising counsel by having greater control of the fundraising operation, typically including conducting the solicitation itself and/or having custody or control of contributions at some time.

Under the Model Solicitations Act (1986), "paid solicitor" means "a person who for compensation performs for a charitable organization any service in connection with which contributions are, or will be, solicited in this state by such compensated person or by any compensated person he employs, procures, or engages, directly or indirectly to solicit. No lawyer, investment counselor or banker who advises a person to make a charitable contribution shall be deemed, as the result of such advice, to be a paid solicitor. A bona fide salaried officer employee or volunteer of a charitable organization shall not be deemed to be a paid solicitor."

As another example, in the North Carolina General Statutes Section 131F-2(10), "solicitor" means "any person who, for compensation, does not qualify as a fund-raising consultant and does either of the following:

a. Performs any service, including the employment or engagement of other persons or services, to solicit contributions for a charitable organization or sponsor.

b. Plans, conducts, manage, consults, whether directly or indirectly, in connection with the solicitation of

contributions for a charitable organization or
sponsor."

Profit
The excess of returns over expenditure in a transaction or
series of transactions

Pre-tax Net Income: A corporation's annual net income
before it has paid taxes. The Internal Revenue Service
currently allows corporations to deduct charitable
contributions as much as 10 percent of their pre-tax net
income.

Philanthropic Advisor: An individual or firm that
provides counseling and evaluative services to donors
before and after grant making decisions.

Private Foundation: A foundation that receives most of its
income from, and is subject to control of, an individual or
other single or limited source. Also, the technical IRS term
for an organization that is tax-exempt under Section
501(c)(3) and classified as a private foundation under the
Internal Revenue Code.

Private Operating Foundation: A legal classification for
an endowed organization that uses its income to operate a
charitable activity, such as a school or camp, rather than to
make grants.

Processed Date: The date the contribution was credited to
the account by the Charitable Gift Fund.

Program officer: A staff member of a foundation who
reviews grant proposals and processes applications for the
board of trustees. Only a small percentage of foundations
have program officers.

Program-related investment (PRI): A loan or other investment (as distinguished from a grant) made by a foundation to another organization for a project related to the foundation's philanthropic purposes and interests

Proposal: A written application, often accompanied by supporting documents, submitted to a foundation or corporate giving program in requesting a grant. Most foundations and corporations do not use printed application forms but instead require written proposals; others prefer preliminary letters of inquiry prior to a formal proposal. Consult published guidelines.

Public Charity: Charitable organizations that qualify as public charities, private operating foundations, or private foundations. A public charity, as defined in Section 509 of the Code identified by the IRS as "not a private foundation", normally receives a substantial part of its income, directly or indirectly, from the general public or from government sources.

Public Foundation: A non-profit organization that receives at least one-third of its annual income from the general public (including government agencies and foundations). Public foundations may make grants or engage in charitable activities.

Q

Qualifying distributions: Expenditures of a private foundation made to satisfy its annual payout requirement. These can include grants, reasonable administrative expenses, set-asides, loans and program-related investments, and amounts paid to acquire assets used directly in carrying out tax-exempt purposes.

Critical Thinking for Critical Times   79

Query letter: A brief letter outlining an organization's activities and its request for funding that is sent to a potential grant maker in order to determine whether it would be appropriate to submit a full grant proposal. Many grant makers prefer to be contacted in this way before receiving a full proposal.

R

Research: "The Code of Federal Regulations defines research as "...a systematic investigation, including research development, testing and evaluation, designed to develop or to contribute to generalized knowledge."

RFP: An acronym for Request for Proposal. When the government issues a new contract or grant program, it sends out RFPs to agencies that might be qualified to participate. The RFP lists project specifications and application procedures. While a few foundations occasionally use RFPs in specific fields, most prefer to consider proposals that are initiated by applicants.

Received Date: The date the contribution was credited to the account by the Charitable Gift Fund for tax purposes.

S

Sarbanes-Oxley Act - officially named the Public Company Accounting Reform and Investor Protection Act of 2002, became law on July 30, 2002. The law was informally named after its sponsors, Senator Paul Sarbanes (D-MD) and Representative Michael G. Oxley (R-OH). The recently enacted Sarbanes-Oxley Act of 2002 includes provisions addressing audits, financial reporting and disclosure, conflicts of interest, and corporate governance at public companies.

Secretary of State

The leader of an executive-branch government agency that usually is responsible for recordation duties. For instance, when establishing a corporation, Articles of Incorporation are typically filed with the Secretary of State for the state in which the corporation is established.

Seed Money: A grant or contribution used to start a new project or organization.

Social welfare

Organized public or private social services for the assistance of disadvantaged groups.

Solicitation, Solicit, Soliciting

Also "charitable solicitation." In the Model Solicitations Act (1986), "Solicit" and "solicitation" mean "the request directly or indirectly for money, credit, property, financial assistance, or other thing of any kind or value on the plea or representation that such money, credit, property, financial assistance, or other thing of any kind or value, or any portion thereof, will be used for a charitable purpose or benefit a charitable organization. Without limiting the scope of the foregoing, these words shall include the following methods of requesting or securing such money, credit, property, financial assistance or other thing of value:

(1) Any oral or written request;

(2) the making of any announcement to the press, over the radio or television or by telephone or telegraph concerning an appeal or campaign by or for any charitable organization or purpose;

(3) the distribution, circulation, posting or publishing of any handbill, written advertisement or other publication which directly or by implication seeks to obtain public support;

(4) the sale of, offer or attempt to sell, any advertisement, advertising space, book, card, tag, coupon, device,

magazine, membership, merchandise, subscription, flower, ticket, candy, cookies or other tangible item in connection with which any appeal is made for any charitable organization or purpose, or where the name of any charitable organization is used or referred to in any such appeal as an inducement or reason for making any such sale, or when or where in connection with any such sale, any statement is made that the whole or any part of the proceeds from any such sale will be used for any charitable purpose or benefit any charitable organization.

A solicitation shall be deemed to have taken place whether or not the person making the same receives any contribution."

Solicitor
For purposes of NPO law, a person or organization that solicits charitable donations (contributions). In some state laws, "solicitor" has the same or a similar meaning as professional solicitor.

Sponsorship: Affiliation with an existing non-profit organization for the purpose of receiving grants. Grant seekers may either apply for federal tax-exempt status or affiliate with a non-profit sponsor.

Standardized Registration Kit
See Uniform Registration Statement.

Statutory law
The body of written law established by enactments expressing the will of legislature, in contrast to common law or case law.

Successor Election: The designation, in writing by a donor, of a person to be assigned the rights and duties associated with the donor's account at the Charitable Gift

Fund upon the donor's death. Successors are eligible only after the deaths of all donors named on the account. The donor designates an individual as the successor, or the donor may choose to recommend that one or more charitable organizations receive the proceeds of any remaining units in the account upon the donor's death.

T

Tax-exempt Organization: A non-profit organization which, because it engages in charitable activities, does not have to pay state or federal taxes. An organization must apply to both the IRS and its state Attorney General's office to receive tax-exempt status.

Trustee: (1) A board member of a foundation. Trustees are responsible for setting foundation policy and making fund decisions. (2) An individual or corporation named to administer the terms of a trust document.

U

Uniform Registration Statement, URS
A form contained in the Standardized Registration Kit, which is accepted by most states that require registration of non-profit organizations conducting charitable solicitations within their jurisdiction, in lieu of each state's own form for this purpose. Some states that will accept the URS require certain supplementary information provided through additional forms included in the Kit. The Standardized Registration Kit, which is sponsored by the National Association of Attorneys General (NAAG) and the National Association of State Charities Officials (NASCO), is available online or in printed form from any of several distributors.

United States Code, USC

A consolidation and codification of the general and permanent laws of the United States arranged by subject under 50 titles, the first six dealing with general or political subjects, and the other 44 alphabetically arranged from agriculture to war. The United States Code is updated annually, and available for online search or download. Commonly abbreviated as U.S. Code, U.S.C. or USC.

V

W

X

Y

Z

Critical Thinking for Critical Times   85

BULK DISCOUNTS

Order for everyone in your Organization!
1-9 copies, $12.99 each
10-24 copies, $9.29 each
25 or more copies $7.29 each
For 100 copies or more copies, contact Divine Publishing @
(501) 339-8042

_____
Name

_____
Title or Department (if any)

_____
Organization

_____
Address

_____
City, State/Province, zip/postal code

_____
E-mail address

_____
Phone

Please send me_____(quantity) Copies   Shipping$_____

Total Amount$_____

Shipping and Handling:
For orders over $100, add 10% of total
For orders $51-$99, add $12
For orders $20-$50, add $7
For orders less then $20, add $4

To Order:
Fax- **(501)-548-6488**   *E-mail* **–info.divinepublishing.org or**
*Website-***www.divinepublishing.org,**
*Mail-***P.O. Box 11073 Conway, AR. 72034**